Maidenhead

IN OLD PHOTOGRAPHS

Maidenhead

IN OLD PHOTOGRAPHS

Collected by MYRA HAYLES *and*
DAVID HEDGES

Alan Sutton Publishing Limited
Phoenix Mill · Far Thrupp
Stroud · Gloucestershire

First published 1992

British Library Cataloguing in Publication Data

Hayles, Myra
  Maidenhead in Old Photographs
  I. Title II. Hedges, David
  942.296

  ISBN 0-7509-0128-4

Typeset in 9/10 Sabon.
Typesetting and origination by
Alan Sutton Publishing Limited.
Printed and bound by
WBC, Bridgend, Mid Glam.

Contents

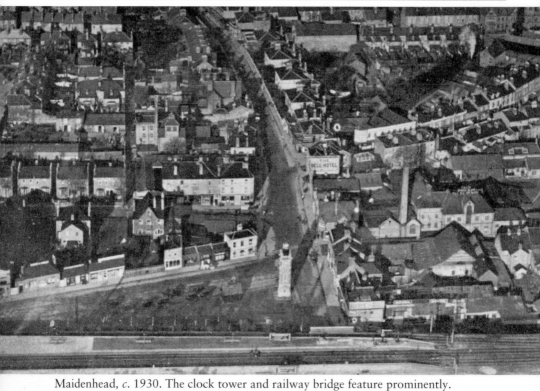

Maidenhead, *c.* 1930. The clock tower and railway bridge feature prominently.

Originally known as New Road, this road was firmly established as Queen Street by the time of this 1904 view.

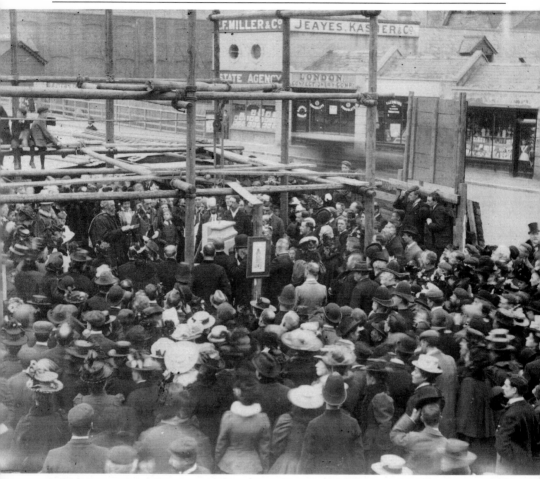

A large crowd assembled to witness the laying of the foundation stone of the clock tower, which commemorated the Diamond Jubilee of the reign of Queen Victoria in 1897.

Two later views of Station Approach featuring the handsome clock which is now a well-known Maidenhead landmark. Mr G.A. Battcock, a notable local resident, generously gave the clock to the town.

King Street, *c.* 1904, with the brewery of W. Nicholson on the right.

Mr William Nicholson was the most prominent of the three local brewers, and he is remembered in the naming of the present shopping precinct, Nicholson's Walk. In his advertisements the brewery was known as the Pineapple Steam Brewery, and was agent for Guinness Stout and Bass and India Pale Ale.

Nicholson's dray was a familiar sight in Maidenhead and the surrounding area.

The premises of Eastman's, the popular Maidenhead photographer.

The site of the Greyhound Inn, proudly recalled in this advertisement of J.C. Webber & Sons, is now the NatWest bank and is signified by a plaque on the wall of the bank.

Generous benefactors, including Mr Andrew Carnegie and Alderman W. Nicholson, contributed to the cost of £6,000 for the library, which opened in 1904. This building was replaced in 1973.

The Sun Inn, Castle Hill, shown on the right with its magnificent portico, was probably the largest of all Maidenhead coaching inns.

Another view of Castle Hill, *c.* 1910, showing The Ice House on the right.

The Ice House, Castle Hill, was erected over ice wells and was originally used by a local fishmonger, Mr Hamblett.

A view of Castle Hill, *c.* 1907.

Two of Maidenhead's cinemas are featured here. Above, the Picture Theatre, Bridge Avenue in 1926, and below, the Rialto Theatre, Bridge Street, which opened in 1928. The Rialto later became the ABC Cinema.

This attractive restaurant was in St Ives Road, formerly Ives Road.

The St Ives Hotel was formerly Ives Place, the mansion of the manor of Ive.

Cullern's Passage ran between Braywick Road and High Street.

Bridge Road from Maidenhead Bridge, Maidenhead.

Bridge House, on the right, and the Riviera Hotel, opposite, are featured in this postcard of Maidenhead Bridge, produced around 1901. This was 'the age of the bicycle' when it was possible to leave the cycle anywhere.

An exterior view of a popular leisure venue, Maidenhead Skating Rink.

The old post office was situated near the Guildhall.

The Memorial to Maidonians who fell in the First World War was in the open space adjoining the town library in St Ives Road.

Lipton's Market was at 72 High Street, and proudly displayed the royal coat of arms ('by appointment to HM The Queen').

Lipton's delivery service pictured before the First World War.

Den Deane of 48 Market Street, photographed at the door of his shoemakers shop.

The notable Maidenhead family of Stuchbery, although originally brewers, opened a store in High Street and also founded the local legal practice.

Smyth's Almshouses in Bridge Street, a beautiful seventeenth-century brick building.

Over the centre archway of the Almshouses is a tablet. The inscription reads 'Theis Almshouses were erected and built at ye sole and proper cost and charges of James Smyth Esquior Citizen and Salter of London in ye year of our Lord 1659.'

The first Maidenhead police station, built in 1857, was situated at the corner of South Street in Broadway, and was replaced in 1906. The later building (shown below) was demolished in 1980.

Looking towards Maidenhead Bridge, *c.* 1907.

Shops at the junction of High Street and Queen Street, *c.* 1881.

The Maidenhead Union premises in St Marks Road were built in 1896.

Dairy delivery carts in St Marks Road.

An early print of Chapel Arches. The stream is now contained within one arch and is known as York Stream.

Maidenhead, Old Toll Gate.

There were toll gates at the Thicket, Braywick Road, Cookham Bridge and Maidenhead Bridge.

The family firm of E.T. Biggs was founded in 1866, the first shop being situated in Queen Street. The business moved to High Street and was patronized by royalty, particularly Queen Mary.

Introduction

Maidenhead In Old Photographs records the changing face of a thriving Thames Valley town that owes its prosperity to excellent communications, by road, river and rail, but whose beginnings were as a small hamlet called South Ellington. About 1280 a wooden bridge replaced the ford across the River Thames and the town started to grow. A staging post was created between London and the West, it being a convenient stopping place just twenty-six miles and a day's ride from London. It was customary for stagecoach travellers to spend the night in Maidenhead rather than face the perils of Maidenhead Thicket, the haunt of highwaymen, in the dark. Linked with Cookham and Bray, the town was already thriving when Queen Elizabeth granted its first charter.

The coming of the railway in 1841 put an end to coaching, and the population had to adjust as the visitors moved in. Maidenhead became a popular commuter town, and many people set up as shopkeepers and tradesmen. In the 1860s a great wave of popularity for the River Thames saw the population double and, before the end of Queen Victoria's reign, double yet again. The banks of the River Thames, and in particular Boulters Lock, are known to millions of people. In the Edwardian period, this section of the river reached the height of its fame as a favourable pleasure resort. The Sunday following the June race meeting at Ascot was the time for the famous to be seen at Boulters Lock, mingling with the officers of the Brigade of Guards whose boat club was established at Maidenhead in about 1865.

The motor car has been a major factor in redevelopment in recent years; as in many other towns, a bypass was created and many places pictured in this book were swallowed up. Offices and parking places now proliferate, and residential areas have been established.

This book is not a history of Maidenhead, but rather a nostalgic trip. The area between the bridge and the Thicket is strong in community pride and many people have contributed photographs, some familiar, others personal, which recall the life of local people engaged in their occupations and leisure activities.

In 1974 Maidenhead joined with Windsor to become the Royal Borough of Windsor and Maidenhead but both communities have continued to retain their individual identities. It is hoped that this pictorial journey into the past will be a reminder of a vanished way of life, and for new arrivals to the town we trust that it will give a glimpse of the working and social life of Maidenhead.

High Street, Maidenhead.

SECTION ONE
The Town

Bridge Street, 1907.

This view of Bridge Street (A4 or Bath Road), *c.* 1907, and the one on the previous page show the tranquillity of the road before the onslaught by the motor car in the twenties and thirties.

Breweries were well represented in Maidenhead, and Horley & Sons were agents for eight of them from their new offices, seen here around 1907, in Station Chambers.

The High Street in the early part of the twentieth century, showing the Bear Hotel on the right.

High Street, *c.* 1906, showing the Town Hall on the left with the Swan Inn on the right and also an early view of R. Martin's, the general draper and ladies-wear shop, in the background.

A.H. Tuffrey & Sons were bakers in Old Post Office Lane, and used this handcart for deliveries in Maidenhead.

A view of Maidenhead High Street in 1925, looking east.

Another part of the High Street, *c.* 1910.

Maidenhead High Street, *c.* 1927, showing S.R. Thompson next to Budgen's, the well-known grocers. Even then the High Street was busy with the traffic of the Bath Road.

SECTION TWO

Personalities and Events

Taplow Court, the home of the Grenfell family, enjoys extensive views of the Thames Valley and Home Counties, and overlooks Cliveden Reach and Boulters Lock.

Lord and Lady Desborough.

Lord and Lady Desborough. Willy Grenfell (1855–1945) married Ettie Fane and was created 1st Baron Desborough. He was one of the most famous all-round athletes of his time and took a strong interest in sporting events. He was Mayor of Maidenhead in 1895 and 1896, and donated land for parks and public buildings. Lord Desborough and his wife lived in Taplow Court.

Lord and Lady Desborough's eldest son, Julian.

Into Battle

The naked earth is warm with spring,
  And with green grass and bursting trees
Leans to the sun's gaze glorying,
  And quivers in the sunny breeze;
And life is colour and warmth and light,
  And a striving evermore for these;
And he is dead who will not fight;
  And who dies fighting has increase.

The fighting man shall from the sun
  Take warmth, and life from the glowing earth;
Speed with the light-foot winds to run,
  And with the trees to newer birth;
And find, when fighting shall be done,
  Great rest, and fullness after dearth.

All the bright company of Heaven
  Hold him in their high comradeship,
The Dog-Star, and the Sisters Seven,
  Orion's Belt and sworded hip.

The woodland trees that stand together,
  They stand to him each one a friend;
They gently speak in the windy weather;
  They guide to valley and ridge's end.

The kestrel hovering by day,
  And the little owls that call by night,
Bid him be swift and keen as they,
  As keen of ear, as swift of sight.

The blackbird sings to him, 'Brother, brother,
  If this be the last song you shall sing,
Sing well, for you may not sing another;
  Brother, sing.'

In dreary, doubtful, waiting hours,
  Before the brazen frenzy starts.
The horses show him nobler powers;
  O patient eyes, courageous hearts!

And when the burning moment breaks,
  And all things else are out of mind,
And only joy of battle takes
  Him by the throat, and makes him blind,

Through joy and blindness he shall know,
  Not caring much to know, that still
Nor lead nor steel shall reach him, so
  That it be not the Destined Will.

The thundering line of battle stands,
  And in the air death moans and sings;
But Day shall clasp him with strong hands,
  And Night shall fold him in soft wings.

Julian Grenfell is one of the best remembered of all the First World War poets. This poem, 'Into Battle', had been sent home to his mother some weeks before he died from wounds received at Ypres in 1915. Before his death, Captain Julian Grenfell of the Royal Dragoons had earned a reputation for bravery and had been awarded the DSO. Lord Desborough's other son, Billy, was also killed in the First World War.

William Nicholson started the Pineapple Brewery in 1840 at the bottom of Nicholson's Lane. He only employed fourteen people in 1856 but by 1936 there were 150. He became a leading citizen, and lived on Castle Hill.

There is no date on this photograph of a very early fire engine, but it was taken before uniforms were issued. The fire brigade was in existence before 1866, and subscriptions were asked for to provide clothing and equipment.

The brigade features in many old photographs and made important contributions to events other than fire fighting.

The fire brigade provided a guard of honour for Queen Victoria's Diamond Jubilee. Mr Budgen, the deputy mayor, was chairman of the Festivities Committee, and was possibly the gentleman standing at the door.

These details from the photograph above highlight a member of the fire brigade and, possibly, Mr Budgen.

Jubilee celebrations. The committee set the programme which included dinner for the elderly (over 55!) at 1 p.m. and tea for the schoolchildren at 4 p.m. Tables were set up in Grenfell Park.

The proclamation of the death of Queen Victoria was read by Mayor William Ferguson Good from the steps of the Town Hall. Note the fire brigade in attendance again, and the boys brigade.

The proclamation of King George V from the same position. This time we see the boy scouts and the armed forces as well as the fire brigade.

Empire shopping day was established to celebrate Queen Victoria's birthday, with the shops specially decorated. There was a competition for the lucky numbers on programmes, which had to be found in the shop windows.

Outside Nicholson and Sons Ltd a very substantial arch of casks was the chief feature for the coronation celebrations.

The *Advertiser* reported that the 'High Street being narrow lends itself to decorative effect, and on this occasion it presented the appearance of one continuous gorgeously adorned triumphal arch.'

Borough of Maidenhead.

CORONATION FESTIVITIES.

In consequence of the unfavourable state of the weather

The Sports are postponed.

The Thanksgiving Service will be held in the Drill Hall.

The Dinner will be held in the Skating Rink.

The Tea to the School Children will be served in the various Schools.

The Baby Show will be held in the Town Hall.

The Variety Entertainments will be held in the Drill Hall.

The above will take place at the times originally arranged and set out in the Official Programme.

W. FERGUSON GOOD,
Mayor.

Guildhall, Maidenhead,
22nd June, 1911.

R. LOOSLEY, PRINTER, 55, QUEEN STREET, MAIDENHEAD.

All contingencies were planned for. This was the first time that a baby show was featured.

The 1947 Borough Council. Front row, left to right: (Aldermen) W.E. Hopgood, E.B. Norris, J.B. Maudsley, Mrs O.P. Frank (mayoress), Dr P.O. Frank (mayor), S. Platt (Town Clerk), Dr W. Doherty, W. Archer, H.H. Neve. The names of many of these leading citizens are still widely recognized.

This delightful picture shows Edgar Neve in his pram at the back of his parents' shop in the High Street.

The exterior of Neve's shop displayed the outfitting goods. Their catalogue illustrated the high quality of their goods.

A Neve family line-up. Top left to bottom right: Madge and Cuthbert, Rupert and Arthur, Alfred, Edgar. The Neves typify the trade families who became involved in the community. Harold became mayor in 1941 and 1942, while his son John followed in 1969.

A Neve family outing to Burnham Beeches for a picnic.

As with many families they suffered tragedy when they lost one of the twins, Rupert, in a flying accident.

Line-up of the First World War volunteers, with Edgar Neve second from the left in the front.

The Second World War wardens shown here include the daughter and son-in-law, Mr and Mrs Vickers, of one of the volunteers in the First World War.

Field Marshal Sir Bernard Law Montgomery waves to the crowd as he rides through the town on his way to receive the freedom of Maidenhead on 19 October 1945.

Field Marshal Montgomery and the mayor, Alderman Oldershaw, were both scholars at St Paul's School, Hammersmith. 'Monty' accepted the freedom after inspecting two guards of honour at Ray Street and the Rialto cinema. He also met twelve mayors from the surrounding towns who were in attendance. He was only the fourth person to receive this honour, the others being Lord Desborough and Alderman Cox in 1919, and Alderman Wesley Walker in 1928.

Alderman Cox learned to drive at the age of 85. He is seen here with his new car which replaced his pony. He was eight times the mayor of Maidenhead.

The food office was opposite the library in St Ives Road. These clerks had to go in a group for security reasons to collect the food coupons and identity cards for distribution. The most convenient transport at that time was a road sweeper's barrow.

John Barker Maudsley CBE, a Yorkshireman, was a member of the borough council from 1936 until his death in 1969. In recognition of his contribution to the town a memorial garden was set up where the old library stood. The large boulder comes from Yorkshire.

The Duchess of Kent can be seen with some of the WVS workers outside the St Ives Hotel canteen during a wartime visit.

A group of prize-winning nurses in the 1950s from the Cottage Hospital, which was founded in 1879. In 1900 A. Waldorf Astor of Cliveden donated £10,000 to celebrate his son's coming of age. The hospital was demolished in 1977.

The front entrance and aerial view of the hospital, which was sited in St Lukes Road.

The *Maidenhead Advertiser*'s outing in the 1950s. It is still a very popular local newspaper and gives support to many events.

Cox's outing to Southend in 1924, which set out from The Foresters at Cox Green.

Alpha Coaches had the reputation for providing excellent services to local villages.

Maidenhead had its own orchestra, which often played to audiences in the Town Hall.

Beating of the Bounds marks the borough boundary every decade, following an adventurous course. The ancient stones, nails or crosses are all checked. Here we see Mr Herbert.

The Lord High Steward's dinner at Taplow Court.

Prince Christian and the Duke of Connaught can be seen leaving the President's tent at the Royal County Show in 1907. It was held at Spencer's Farm, North Town, and was described as having a miniature wooden city with a central ring, where the animals were paraded and the show-jumping took place. The show was founded in 1861 and enjoyed royal support.

SECTION THREE

The River

Boulters Lock, undoubtedly the most famous of all the locks on the River Thames, at the turn of the century. Its equally famous lock keeper, Mr W.H. Turner, is seen here in charge of proceedings on the right of the picture. W.H. Turner and Mr W.H. Grenfell (later Lord Desborough) of Taplow Court, were both influential in making Maidenhead one of the most popular resorts in the south of England. Ascot Sunday was one of the busiest days of the year, when the rich and famous flocked to Boulters, not only to be seen in their Ascot finery, but to take river trips in the electric launches, skiffs and punts of the period. William Turner was an ex-naval gunner, one of a number of ex-naval personnel employed as lock keepers by the Thames Conservancy at this time. He was probably the best known character on the river, and apart from his skill in packing the river craft into the lock, he was responsible for saving the lives of many people from drowning during his period at Boulters. His lock garden won many prizes while he was lock keeper at Boulters.

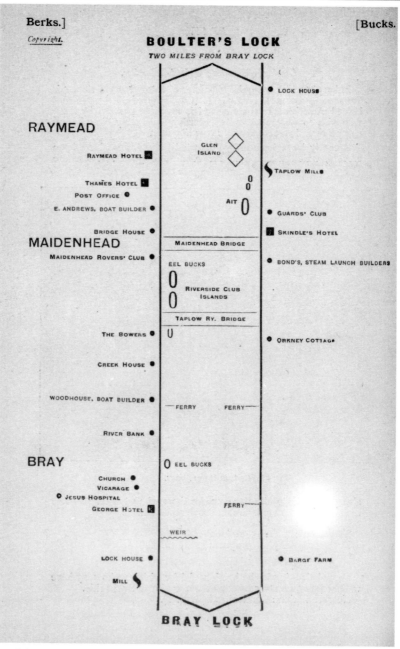

A plan of the River Thames between Boulters Lock and Bray Lock, *c.* 1903.

Ray Mills, *c.* 1910, situated by Boulters Lock. Ray Mills was in use until the early part of the twentieth century. Shortly after this photograph was taken it was demolished.

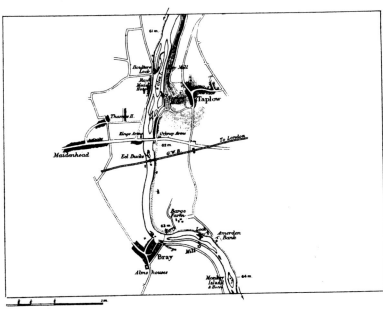

Henry Taunt's map of the River Thames from Oxford to London was surveyed in 1871, and this is the section between Boulters Lock and Bray Lock.

An aerial view of Boulters Lock, *c.* 1930. Cliveden Reach, between Boulters and Cookham Locks, has been described by many writers as the finest scenery in the whole of the Thames Valley.

The weir at Boulters.

The boat transit at Boulters Lock was installed in 1912, when the lock was enlarged, and replaced a much earlier trolley road. Before the First World War, in the heyday of the river, it was quite usual for over 1,000 small craft and launches to use Boulters Lock on a single summer Sunday.

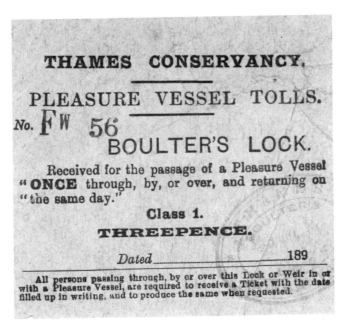

THAMES CONSERVANCY,

PLEASURE VESSEL TOLLS.

No. FW 56

BOULTER'S LOCK.

Received for the passage of a Pleasure Vessel "**ONCE** through, by, or over, and returning on "the same day."

Class 1.
THREEPENCE.

*Dated*_____189

All persons passing through, by or over this Lock or Weir in or with a Pleasure Vessel, are required to receive a Ticket with the date filled up in writing, and to produce the same when requested.

A toll ticket, showing that everyone passing through the lock was charged the same toll.

River craft leaving and entering Boulters. Ascot Sunday was particularly popular, and it became part of the social calendar for the wealthy and famous to be seen at Boulters Lock.

615 MAIDENHEAD. — *Thames Hotel.* — LL.

The Thames Hotel was built in the 1880s. The proprietor, Mr H. Woodhouse, was a well-known boat hirer and builder. The Thames Hotel rivalled Skindles in its popularity and Mr Woodhouse was a popular host, his speciality being silver eels. He was a pioneer in the hiring of punts, canoes and other river craft from his boat-houses at Maidenhead Court and Bray.

Bonds were very early boat builders in Maidenhead and, with Mr Woodhouse of the Thames Hotel, were among the first to make the hiring of boats an important local industry. Together with Wilder and Andrews, these two local businesses prospered during the 'Golden Age' of the River Thames.

View of the river from Wilder's boat-house on a busy Ascot Sunday.

Maidenhead Court boat-house, owned by Mr H. Woodhouse, proprietor of the Thames Hotel.

This Wilder's advertisement illustrates the range of river craft available for hire.

Maidenhead's elegant bridge was designed by Sir Robert Taylor and opened in 1772, replacing the earlier wooden structure.

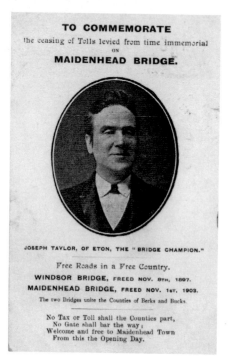

TO COMMEMORATE
the ceasing of Tolls levied from time immemorial
ON
MAIDENHEAD BRIDGE.

JOSEPH TAYLOR, OF ETON, THE "BRIDGE CHAMPION."

Free Roads in a Free Country.

WINDSOR BRIDGE, FREED NOV. 8TH, 1897.
MAIDENHEAD BRIDGE, FREED NOV. 1ST, 1903.

The two Bridges unite the Counties of Berks and Bucks.

No Tax or Toll shall the Counties part,
No Gate shall bar the way;
Welcome and free to Maidenhead Town
From this the Opening Day.

Tolls were levied for over six hundred years until 1903, when the campaign of Mr Joseph Taylor of Eton resulted in the ending of tolls and the gates being thrown in the river.

Maidenhead Bridge from the Buckinghamshire bank, with the Riviera Hotel on the Berkshire shore. Built as a mansion, the Riviera was converted into a hotel in the 1880s to cater for the increasing number of visitors.

River sports and Venetian fêtes were regular events in many Thames-side resorts. Mr W.H. Grenfell (later Lord Desborough) of Taplow Court was a keen supporter of all activities on the Thames, and was amateur punting champion.

The most popular event on the river was the regatta.

The name of Skindles is synonymous with Maidenhead, despite the fact that it is situated on the Buckinghamshire bank of the River Thames. Originally known as the Orkney Arms, the name taken from the then owner of Taplow Court, it was a small coaching inn on the Bath Road. Soon after the Great Western Railway reached Slough, the inn was taken over by Mr Skindle, and, having purchased adjoining land, he erected new premises.

This most famous of all riverside hotels soon became a popular haunt for the rich and famous during the heyday of the river. It was probably for this reason that Jerome K. Jerome in his classic of the Thames, *Three Men In A Boat* (1889), did not rate Maidenhead too highly when he wrote: 'Maidenhead itself is too snobby to be pleasant. It is the town of showy hotels, patronised chiefly by dudes and ballet girls. It is the witches kitchen from which go forth those demons of the river – steam launches.' He concluded by saying, 'We went through Maidenhead quickly, and then eased up, and took leisurely that grand reach beyond Boulters and Cookham Locks.'

Maidenhead Bridge

During the last century eel bucks were sited at various points on the river, and those at Maidenhead remained until the early years of this century.

Cliveden House, nestling in the trees above Cliveden Reach, dates from 1851, the two previous houses on the site having been destroyed by fire. It is best remembered as the house of the Astor family and the centre of the 'Cliveden set' – as members of Lord and Lady Astor's house parties were known.

Salter's steamer, *Cliveden*, seen here passing Cliveden House, *c.* 1910. Salter's of Oxford is still the major Thames passenger boat operator, being founded in the 1870s.

Above, an early photograph of Cliveden Reach, and below, Cliveden Cottage and woods, both practically unchanged today.

My Lady ferry at Cliveden Reach, *c*. 1900, was used solely by bargees for moving their horses where the towpath changed from one shore to the other.

Botany Bay, Maidenhead, a mooring for houseboats during the early part of the century.

King Edward VII with a party at Monkey Island, *c.* 1908.

The George Hotel and ferry, Bray.

A view of Bray from the river.

BOURNE END

Townsend Bros. were important boat builders of all types of river craft.

Bourne End was notable for its many sailing craft and for Bourne End Sailing Week, held in June each year.

Maidenhead Bridge and Bridge House.

A view of Raymead, Maidenhead before the First World War.

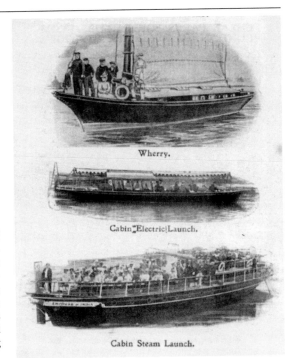

Wherry.

Cabin Electric Launch.

Cabin Steam Launch.

Examples of the many types of river craft available for hire during the Edwardian era. Keith Prowse were agents for the complete holiday or excursion on the Thames, and their *River Thames Guide* for the period covers everything from catering and hotels to the hire of camping equipment.

The Riviera Hotel was originally built as a riverside mansion for letting, but this proved to be unsuccessful and it opened as a hotel in 1891.

The George Hotel at Bray was a popular venue.

Taplow, with Sounding Arch in the background.

Between the wars and into the 1940s and '50s the Hotel de Paris at Bray was a favourite spot.

A later picture of *My Lady* ferry at Cliveden Reach.

Floods in 1928 and 1947. In common with many Thames-side towns, Maidenhead has suffered through the years with periodic flooding, the last serious occurrence being in 1947. It is therefore appropriate to remember that while this is considered an area of pleasure and recreation, the river can also cause suffering and hardship on occasions, as the four final pictures of this section confirm.

Flooding in Maidenhead.

Transport

Maidenhead's first railway station, situated on the Bath Road at Taplow, was opened in 1838.

The Great Western Railway reached the Buckinghamshire side of the Thames at Taplow in 1838, and the first wooden station building was situated opposite the Dumb Bell Inn on the Bath Road. It was known as Riverside station. By 1839 Brunel's bridge was completed, and the line opened to Twyford.

Riverside station served Maidenhead until 1854, when a new station, known as Boyn Hill, was erected on Castle Hill. Both Boyn Hill and Riverside were closed in 1871 when the present station opened.

Castle Hill, *c.* 1907, showing the disused entrance to Boyn Hill station.

A Brooklands School of Flying aeroplane on the opening day of Maidenhead Aerodrome in June 1929. Situated at the junction of Windsor Road and Holyport Road, the site eventually became a nursery and later a small housing development.

A British bus to Reading, near the Seven Stars on the Bath Road, seen here in 1916. British buses were the forerunners of Thames Valley buses.

King Edward VII was a frequent visitor to Maidenhead.

A twenty-seater bus belonging to West Bros. of Bray, waiting outside Maidenhead railway station. This bus operated between Bray and Maidenhead from 1927 to 1938.

An early Carter's Alpha Coach.

Motor taxis replaced the one-horse flies at the cab rank in Station Approach. These operated within the town and to villages around.

Maidenhead's first motor accident?

A Grenfell Coach owned by Mr G.W. Collins of 4 Grenfell Road.

One of the well-known Three Lilies buses. Near the Bear Hotel and the Rialto cinema was the main starting and setting down point for the Thames Valley, and numerous other private bus companies which served the outer areas of Maidenhead and surrounding villages.

Two Thames Valley buses negotiating a flooded Bridge Road during the floods of 1947.

An Alpha Coach belonging to Carters of Maidenhead, at Ascot Racecourse in the 1930s.

The British Automobile Traction Co. Ltd, forerunners of Thames Valley Bus Services, operated the first bus service in Maidenhead from 1915 to 1920. The first bus garage opened in 1916 at 44 Bridge Street. The site was occupied by a large house called The Cedars, part of which was retained for use as offices. The garage, photographed above in the 1930s, was known as The Cedars for many years.

Maidenhead bus station in the 1950s.

A busy scene on the forecourt of Maidenhead station *c.* 1907, after the arrival of a train. The fare table for one-horse flies was published in the official guide to Maidenhead: they served the large area from Wargrave and Henley to Hawthorn Hill. A fare and a half was charged after midnight, and cabs to race meetings, fêtes and any place of amusement had to be booked by special arrangement. Many local businesses can be seen in the background, including the chimney of Nicholson's brewery.

SECTION FIVE

Leisure and Sports

The Wanderers. This 1890 club group is sitting in front of the grandstand at Kidwells Park. It changed its name at least three times, having started as a combined cycling and athletics club.

Maidenhead has been prominent in the development of the cycle, and one of the earliest boneshakers was manufactured by Mr Timberlake. The family ran a cycle shop in Queen Street and in 1870 established the Pilot Cycle Co. Ltd.

A sports day in 1911 to celebrate the coronation of King George V.

Unity Sports - 1911.

Maidenhead Unity Sports again, but this time the trade bicycle race. Note the clothing of the cyclists compared with the 'serious' rider acting as a starting help.

Another example of the enthusiasm for cycling: a trip from London to Bath and back by club members in 1910.

A cricket club at the park. The first report of cricket played in Berkshire is recorded at Maidenhead – in the *Daily Chronicle* of 22 June 1793. In 1894 a Century match was played against the MCC in the ground of Orkney College.

The modern cricket club dates from 1849. A match between an All England Eleven and a Maidenhead Eighteen had the home team winning by eleven runs. William Nicholson was one of the heroes of the match. Alderman Cox can be seen between the two ladies.

A Pinkneys Green eleven in the 1930s.

Bowling was, and still is, a popular sport in Maidenhead. The clothing since 1910 may have changed, but the enthusiasm continues.

The rowing club, founded in 1876, continues to attract members. This group proudly shows off its trophies.

A scout camp at The Thicket.

A 1932 scout group.

The river has not been popular for swimming, and it was not until 1876, when the first baths were opened by the side of the Hambletonian Hall, that a swimming club was established.

Maidenhead Football Club, 1911–12. It was founded in 1870 and had fifteen players a side at first. It joined with the Norfolkian's FC in 1919 to form the Maidenhead United FC.

The shooting range. In 1906, after a visit from Lord Roberts, a civilian rifle club was formed. The range was close to the railway station and golf links.

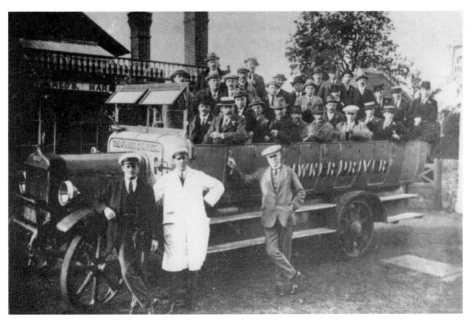

Many coach trips used the Pond House as a starting place.

This picture shows the skating rink in 1910. The building later became the Hippodrome.

Maidenhead Union Rugby Football Club was founded in 1922 and was initially called Thames Valley. It started at Bray horse show grounds and then moved to Kidwells Park. The changing rooms were in the Swan Inn, where the narrow spiral staircase was reputed to cause more injuries than the game itself. In 1966 it moved to Braywick. In the mid-1950s the club began to prosper, and Ray Bonberry, who became the first fixture secretary and team secretary, is seen here on the left of the back row with a young Stirling Moss standing next to him.

There is still a thriving mini and junior section catering for 5–17-year-olds. This photograph shows the 1980 team with Geoff Cowen, their coach.

Schools and Churches

The drill hall and technical school in Marlow Road. The art school was designed by
E.J. Shrewsbury, who was the architect for the clock tower and many of the churches.

St Paul's choir. The church was in High Town Road and was designed by E.J. Shrewsbury. It was the chapel of ease of All Saints' church.

At this garden party for St Luke's church there is a well-known resident, Nurse Chambers, who used to ride around the town on her tricycle. She is the lady with the large bow. St Luke's was created as a district chapelry out of the parish of Cookham.

All Saints' church was consecrated in 1857 on land given by Mr Charles Grenfell. The tower and spire were erected in 1866–7.

St Mary's church was in existence as early as 1324, when it was a chapel. In 1724 it was rebuilt, still in the middle of the road, but moved to its present site in 1824. The present church, with its fibreglass spire, was consecrated in 1965.

The Salvation Army had a visit from General Booth in 1907.

A young class from around 1915 outside the doorway to the East Street Church of England School. This later became St Luke's.

A later, older group in the same place at the East Street School. The sashes denote the grades that the pupils have reached.

This is probably the earliest photograph in existence of the whole of the County School, founded in 1894. It is dated 1899.

The County School moved to Shoppenhangers Road. Part of the curriculum was to practise digging redoubts.

Members of the County School during a very formal PE competition.

The same school, but now a grammar school, and a light-hearted approach to games with this 'boat' race.

Here we see the boys from the County School digging the rifle range on the west side of the football field. The Army Cadet Corps was an important part of school life.

Acting in the Modern School, now Newlands, when *The Critic* was performed in December 1906.

A young actor from the County School.

The County Boys' Grammar is now Desborough, a grant maintained school. Its centenary is in 1994.

Sport has always been well represented, and this is a schoolboys' boxing team.

Gordon Road School has reunions on a regular basis. It was formed when the British and Wesleyan schools were merged.

A group of teachers from Gordon Road School in the '50s.

An infant group of the Wesleyan School, *c.* 1927. It stood on the corner of the High Street and Kings Street.

Elmslie School taught members of many local Maidenhead families. The following have so far been identified from the photograph: Bassil, Cox, Dillaway, Frank, Jones, Keats, Lemon, Miller, Saunders, Smith, Stuchbery, Prior, Westlake, Wiltshire.

Miss Theaker and Miss Saunders were joint principals of this private day and boarding school.

A May Day celebration at Ellington School in 1953. The school's diamond anniversary was in 1992.

A coronation cake for the children in the Queen's Street area, held by Mrs Piercey of the Queen's Arms.

SECTION SEVEN

Round About Maidenhead

CAB FARES

FROM MAIDENHEAD STATION (ONE HORSE FLY, including the Driver).

	s.	d.
Ascot ...	11	6
Bisham	4	6
Boulter's Lock	2	0
Boyne Hill Church	1	6
Bray ...	2	0
Burnham	5	0
Burnham Beeches ...	6	6
Castle Hill ...	1	6
Cliveden	6	6
Cookham	4	0
Cookham Dean	5	0
Dropmore	7	0
Furze Platt ...	2	6
Hawthorne Hill	6	6
Henley	11	6
Maidenhead Bridge	2	0
Maidenhead Court...	2	6
Maidenhead Thicket (over)	4	0
Maidenhead Thicket (Heath Court)	2	6
Maidenhead Town...	1	0
Monkey Island	4	0
Ray Mead	2	0
Skindle's Hotel	2	0
Taplow Court	3	6
Thames Hotel	2	0
Wargrave	10	0
Windsor	7	6
Winter Hill ...	6	6

Half the above fares for return journey. A fare and a half is charged after Midnight. To races, fêtes and other places of amusement the hiring must be by special agreement.

POSTAL ARRANGEMENTS

(1st May to 30th September).

MAIDENHEAD POST OFFICE.—Open from 7 a.m. to 9 p.m. daily. Sundays, 8 to 10 a.m. and 5 to 6 p.m.

TELEGRAPH.—From 8 a.m. to 9 p.m. daily. Sundays, 8 to 10 a.m. and 5 to 6 p.m.

There are Four Deliveries, 7 and 10.30 a.m., 3.15 and 6.15 p.m.

Box for London Despatches closes 2.30, 8.45, 11 a.m. and 1.15, 3.55, 4.30 and 9.15 p.m. Sundays, 2.30 a.m. and 9.30 p.m.

THAMES BRANCH OFFICE.—Open for despatch of all Postal and Telegraph Business as follows: Week days, 8 a.m. to 8 p.m. Sundays, 8 to 10 a.m. and 5 to 6 p.m.

C. C. R. TWIST, Esq., Postmaster.

RAILWAY FARES.

FORTNIGHTLY SEASON TICKETS are issued from Paddington to Maidenhead at the following rates:—
First Class, 40/-; Second Class, 29/6; Third Class, 23/-.

RETURN TICKETS, available for six months, are also issued from and to Paddington—First Class, 6/-; Second, 3/9; Third, 3/-; and most of the London Stations on the Metropolitan and District Railway—First Class, 5/6; Second, 4/-; Third, 3/3.

CHEAP DAY RETURN TICKETS, available to return by any train after 4 p.m., are also issued from the same Stations by specified trains on certain days. Third Class Fares, 2/6.

A guidebook of 1907 showing the cab and railway fares and postal arrangements in operation at the time.

Silchester House in the 1920s. It was originally a boarding as well as a day school.

Taplow church had an ancient tumulus in its churchyard. It originally stood close to the mansion.

Somersham Hotel was sited in Ray Park Avenue among three-and-a-half acres of ground.

Shoppenhanger Manor after a fire in 1931.

The Waggon and Horses can still be found at Pinkneys Green, although not the original building. It overlooks National Trust land and a cricket field.

Ockwell Manor House is a very good example of the half-timbered buildings of the Middle Ages, and lies two miles to the south of Maidenhead.

Bray is well known for the song 'The Vicar of Bray'. Apparently, he changed his religion three times rather than surrender his living. Here we see the main village street with the church of St Michael in the background. The church dates from the reign of Edward I, and possesses many beautiful old brasses.

The Hinds Head in Bray was frequented by many famous people.

The Fishery. When Mrs Annie Smith moved here it was the only building apart from a boathouse on Bray Reach. She is remembered for giving annual feasts to the poor.

Jesus Hospital in Bray.

Bray took in all the land to the south of the Bath Road.

Boys Class. Spanish Children's Home, Bray Court.

The Spanish Children's Home was sited at Bray Court, and is seen here around 1938. The children are thought to be evacuees from the Spanish Civil War.

The opening of Bray Airfield in 1929.

A biplane from Brooklands School of Flying.

The Almshouses in Bray were founded by William Goddard and completed in 1628. He left lands to the Fishmongers' Company of London to provide for six poor persons of the parish of Bray.

Cliveden, *c.* 1790. The Cliveden estate was bought by William Waldorf Astor, who later became Lord Astor, in 1893. Later he gave it to his son as a wedding present.

Cockmarsh is a flood plain near Cookham which sometimes froze over to provide skating.

As an ancient borough, Cookham took in all of Maidenhead to the north side of the Bath Road. It is now a popular riverside village.

The Household Brigade Steeplechases

Will take place at

HAWTHORN HILL

(Between Bracknell & Maidenhead),

ON FRIDAY AND SATURDAY,
April 10th and 11th,

UNDER NATIONAL HUNT RULES.

SECOND DAY.

The following race closes by 10 p.m. on TUESDAY NEXT, MARCH 17TH, to A. R. TROTTER, ESQ., 2nd Life Guards, Cavalry Barracks, Windsor.

THE FARMERS' STEEPLECHASE of 40 sov. to the winner, 10 sov. to the second, and 5 sov. to the third (given by the Household Brigade Racing Club); entrance, free; for horses the property on and since January 1st, 1896, of bonâ-fide Farmers either at present occupying, or who have occupied, since January 1st, 1895, land over which the Household Brigade Draghounds, Mr. Garth's Foxhounds, or the Berks and Bucks Farmers' Harriers hunt; four-years-old 11st., five 12st., six and aged 12st. 7lb.; a winner in 1895 or 1896 of any steeplechase to carry 7lb., of two steeplechases 14lb. extra; maiden five-years-old and upwards allowed 7lb.; professional riders 7lb. extra; ten entries, or the race may be void; about two miles and a half.

Colours must be sent with entry.

Clerks of the Course and Stakeholders, MESSRS. PRATT & Co., 9, George Street, Hanover Square, London, W.

Hon. Sec., MAJOR ARC... CRAWLEY Guards' Club,

After the Second World War Hawthorn Hill became the only pony race track in the country, following the closure of the famous Northolt Park. Racing continued until the early 1960s. The golf range and course now occupy the area.

Formosa Island is near Cookham lock, facing the hanging woods of Cliveden.

Monkey Island is so called because the third Duke of Marlborough erected a fishing lodge on the island and had it painted with figures of monkeys.

Dawson's 1837 map of Maidenhead shows its main road, but very little else. The railway line, which opened to Twyford after the completion of Brunel's bridge, can be seen.

Acknowledgements

Although many of the postcards and photographs reproduced in this book are from our own collections we must also acknowledge with thanks the help from local friends and organizations in its compilation – especially the following:

Maidenhead Public Library, in particular Mrs Patricia Curtis and Mrs Rowena Perry who searched through the archives and gave us much encouragement
The *Maidenhead Advertiser*, Mr D.J. Seals, the editor, and Mrs Powell
The sales manager of Berkshire Library and Information Service, Mr N. Bond
Rosemary Addy and Ruth Jenkins of Slough Public Library
Mr and Mrs Atkinson • Mr E.A.S. Brooks • Mr E. Burden • Mr Geoff Cowen of Maidenhead Rugby Club • Mr John Davidson of Miscellania
Mr T. Deadman of the Thames and District Cycling Club
Mr and Mrs D. Holloway • Mr G. Honeyfield of The Attic, Henley
Mrs J. Hunter for the Windsor and Maidenhead Royal Borough Collection
Mrs Pam Knight • Mr Elias Kupfermann of 'Middle Thames Historic Consultants' • Mr Paul Lacey • Mr and Mrs P. Lindley • Mrs R. Piercey
Mr E. Sammes • Mr David Stroud • Mrs E.K. Vickers • Mr Richard Way, bookseller of Henley • Mr R.S.J. Wells of the Waggon and Horses • Mr R. Woolmer of Desborough School.

We have made every effort to establish copyright and have obtained permission to reproduce when required, but if we have inadvertently omitted to do so for any photograph we offer our sincere apologies.
Lastly, for their patience and support, we thank our respective families.